THE FREDDIE MERCURY

TRIBUTE
CONCERT FOR AIDS AWARENESS

International Music Publications Limited
Southend Road, Woodford Green, Essex IG8 8HN, England

❝ We have lost the greatest and most beloved member of our family. We feel overwhelming grief that he has gone, sadness that he should be cut down at the height of his creativity, but above all great pride in the courageous way that he lived and died. It has been a privilege for us to have shared such magical times. As soon as we are able we would like to celebrate his life in the style to which he was accustomed. ❞

John Deacon, Brian May and Roger Taylor, 25th November 1991

On behalf of Freddie.
Thank you to every artist, manager and untold friends worldwide who have helped to make this event possible. We hope that your efforts will enable us to achieve our aim of increasing worldwide awareness and understanding of the threat of AIDS.

Queen, Jim Beach and all at Queen Productions, April 1992

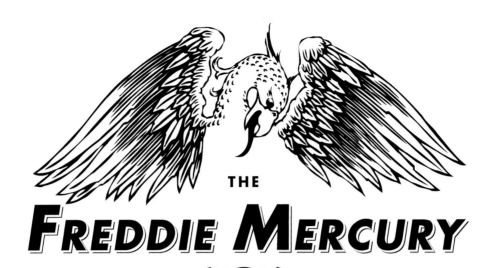

THE
FREDDIE MERCURY
TRIBUTE
CONCERT FOR AIDS AWARENESS

In memory
of the incomparable

FREDDIE MERCURY
1946 - 1991

First published in Great Britain in 1993
by International Music Publications Ltd.

Produced and designed by Richard Gray.

Photographs by :
Neal Preston
Phil Dent
Richard Young (Rex Features),
SIPA (Rex Features)
Mike Putland (Retna Pictures).

ISBN 0 86359 979 6

Printed in England by Hill Shorter Ltd.

International Music Publications Ltd.
Southend Road
Woodford Green
Essex IG8 8HN
England

The Freddie Mercury Tribute Concert
has also been released on video in the
UK and Europe by Picture Music
International on the 23rd November
1992, on video and laser disc in Japan
by VideoArts on 10th December
1992, and on video and laser disc in
North America by Buena Vista Home
Video on 20th April 1993.
A mini-album featuring George
Michael, Queen and Lisa Stansfield,
called Five Live, including tracks from
the Freddie Mercury Tribute has been
released on 20th April 1993 in the UK
by Parlophone Records and in North
America by Hollywood Records.

CONTENTS

THE

FREDDIE MERCURY

TRIBUTE

SOLD OUT
THANK YOU ALL

CONCERT FOR AIDS AWARENESS
Profits to Aids Charities Worldwide

EASTER MONDAY APRIL 20th 1992

WEMBLEY STADIUM

Gates open 3.30pm   Show starts 6.00pm   Show finishes approx. 9.00pm

General Admission £25
A limited number of Reserved Seats at £30 and £35 available only by calling 081 862 0202

Personal callers welcome at Wembley Box Office and at Virgin Megastore Oxford St. & Marble Arch
also Allders of Croydon, Allders of Sutton, Bentalls of Kingston, and all branches of Keith Prowse

CREDIT CARD HOTLINES
Wembley Stadium 081 900 1234 / 071 240 7200 / 071 379 6131 / 071 836 4114
071 734 8932 / 071 580 3141

Limit of 6 tickets per person
(All tickets subject to booking fee except for personal callers at Wembley Box Office)
INFORMATION LINE (0891) 500 255 (calls charged at 36p cheap rate, 48p other times)

Concert produced by Queen and Harvey Goldsmith Entertainments   © 1992 Queen Productions Ltd.

Tickets for the concert sold out in 6 hours

THE MERCURY PHOENIX TRUST

Freddie Mercury died of AIDS related causes in London on 24th November 1991. Immediately afterwards the remaining members of Queen decided to set about raising money and awareness for AIDS in his memory. The Mercury Phoenix Trust was founded to distribute the money raised by the Freddie Mercury Tribute Concert for AIDS Awareness, which took place on 20th april 1992, and the subsequent video and record releases. It is now a registered charity.

Following the concert, hundreds of applications for monetary support were received and are still being dealt with.

Funds generated in the USA through Fox Television's prime time broadcast of the concert (a sum of $853,000) were directly distributed to AIDS charities all over the States, not including $300,000 separately donated to The Magic Johnson Foundation through sales of the Bohemian Rhapsody single.

In addition the Trust has distributed £428,000 to 32 different established charities and Body Positive self-help groups in the UK, Europe, Romania and Africa. This is in addition to a sum in excess of £1,000,000 donated to The Terrence Higgins Trust in London. Collaboration has been realised with groups as far removed as the World Health Organisation to grass-root organisations run by voluntary workers in Uganda. The Trust has concentrated on care for the affected and training for carers. It has also helped with educational projects aimed at young people and especially those in unfortunate circumstances. The Trust is looking into a number of research projects at present.

A number of small donations and requests for information on how people can help have been received. Donations to The Mercury Phoenix Trust are always welcome as it is clear that AIDS charities are badly underfunded. It has become involved with a newly formed charity based in Texas called the Freddie Mercury – Keep Yourself Alive Fund and there are several fledgling local Freddie Mercury charities in Japan and other parts of the world. The Trust is continuing some of its own fundraising activities and intends to keep AIDS awareness in the foreground through the use of Freddie Mercury's name, magic and music.

For donations please contact:
The Mercury Phoenix Trust
Mr. Peter Chant
c/o Queen Productions
46 Pembridge Road
London W11 3HN

Dear Friends

Thank you for joining us.
This concert is for you – we
hope you enjoy it!
It is primarily a celebration
of, and a tribute to, our dear
friend and colleague –
Freddie Mercury.
It is also a means of using the
tragedy of his death to some
good effect in bringing a
greater awareness of the fact
that Aids affects all of us:-
rich, poor, famous, not-
famous, young, old, black,
white, red, yellow, gay or
straight.
This is an important message,
especially for the younger
people of the world, and
especially now!
If the death of Freddie
Mercury can add to this
awareness, it will be a major
addition to the already
wonderful achievements of his
life.
we thank the cast; in every
sense of the word – the best!

Long Live Freddie

(he would have loved all this fuss)

Roger Taylor, *April 1992*

John Deacon, Roger Taylor and Brian May

Roger Taylor

Brian May

John Deacon

Today, we will all be coping with our own memories of Freddie; it's hard to imagine being here without him. Freddie meant a lot of different things to different people – he had a vision of greatness for the band and saw it through. As a perfectionist he always wanted the best and got the best for the band. He was always sensitive to and aware of all the people around him. His sense of fairness encouraged a balance within the band giving room for our own individual creativity and songwriting. Freddie always created a reaction – no one was indifferent to him. We will all miss him.

John Deacon, *April 1992*

It seems inconceivable that we now have to do without Freddie; this proud, vibrant, irreverent and passionately creative man surely cannot have been extinguished in the prime of his life? Freddie was denied the privilege of growing old, but in 45 years he packed in enough living for a dozen lifetimes.

A child of strict upbringing, he was, when I met him some 25 years ago, an uncertain youth stepping into an unfamiliar world outside, but his head was full of great dreams and the certainty that they could be achieved. At the age of 20 he already lived the dreams, and behaved with a gentle grandeur that demanded respect. He looked and acted like a million dollars, though he had scarcely the bus fare home on his person. (that never changed! – later when his millions were safely in the bank, someone else always carried the purse!) Perhaps in changing his name just prior to our first record sleeve, he decided to leave the fragile Frederick Bulsara at home under parental care, and became the God Freddie Mercury.

Freddie was a very uncommon creature in our time – a free spirit. He knew what he wanted to be and set about it with complete dedication. His loves were music and life, life was for living and enjoying to the full, and when life disappointed and hurt him, he poured all the more passion into perfecting his music, the weaving of his spells. He never hid in modesty. He gave himself credit for his own achievements and gave credit generously to the achievements of those around him. Freddie never did anything by halves, he had no time for anything but the best.

His spirit will live on as long as musicians strive to pour excitement, drama and mystery into their work.

I was fortunate to share in many moments of creation with Freddie, and I still hear his voice whenever a mediocre compromise is threatened "No Darling, we *don't* compromise"

His songs say it all *The March Of The Black Queen, Lily Of The Valley, Killer Queen, Bohemian Rhapsody, We Are The Champions, The Miracle, Play The Game,* and many others all have the finest shades of emotion among the bold strokes. Freddie never wanted to discuss his lyrics; "They should speak for themselves" was his curt dismissal.

But the imagination in those lyrics compiled with a magical sense of melody, and a deft knack of sliding between keys at the drop of a hat, made him one of the truly original songwriters of our time. Person, writer and finally performer. This is where the superlatives run out. For, on a stage in front of 200 people or 200,000 he was, of course, matchless. Somehow by channelling his inner self through the heroic, yet intensely human figure that he had created, he reached out to every heart, every boy who ever struggled to be a man, every woman who wanted a man like this. He had the touch of genius which spurred us all to greatness.

Freddie, you did it; you were the best; you changed the world.

God speed.

Brian May, *April 1992*

FREDDIE MERCURY
●
FREE SPIRIT

Roger Taylor and Brian May at rehearsal

The Finale

James Hetfield, Metallica

Jason Newsted, Metallica

❝ We feel they have been one of the most important bands, but have been greatly overlooked and underrated during the last ten years, especially in the States. Their early records had great layered guitar work that sounded like orchestration without the orchestra. They opened our eyes to textures and harmonies.

Hopefully, this concert will open the eyes of a lot of young kids today to understand and appreciate how great and influential Queen were, and still are. ❞

Metallica, *April 1992*

Kirk Hammett, Metallica

Extreme

Gary Cherone, Extreme

Gary Cherone, Extreme

" If I was gonna write a fantasy script to my life, I still couldn't dream up a day at Wembley with Queen. As far as the band, Spiritual, gifted, dramatic, soulful, a musical library !"

Nuno Bettencourt, *April 1992*

Nuno and Brian at rehearsals

Nuno Bettencourt backstage

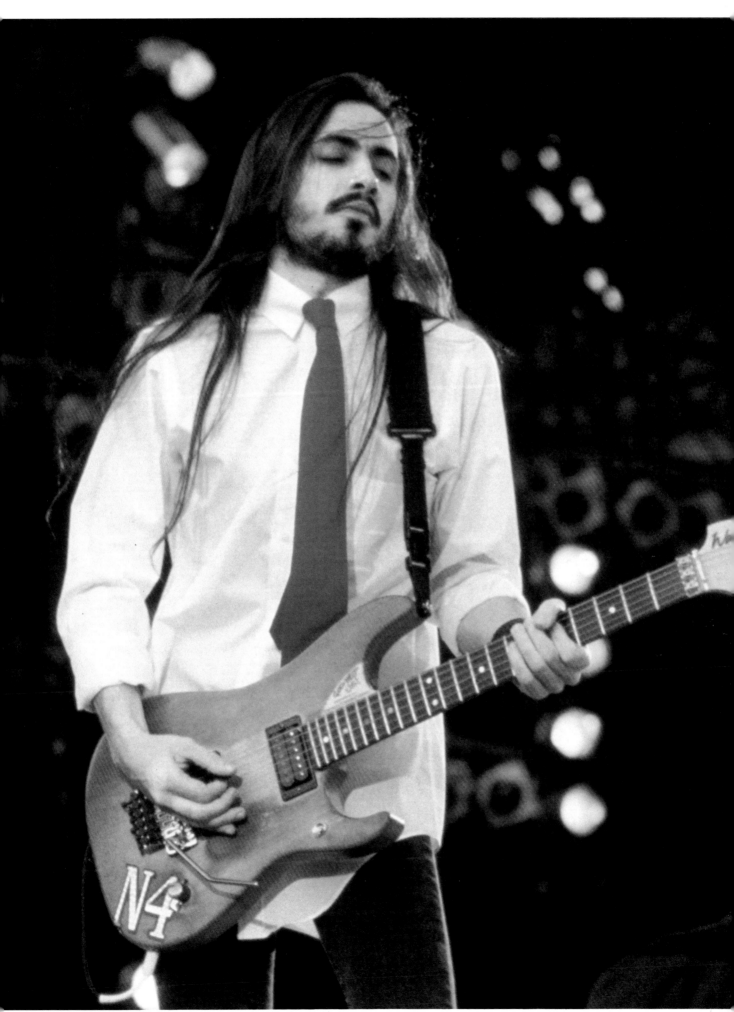

Gary Cherone and Nuno Bettencourt, Extreme

Joe Elliott, Def Leppard

Rick Allen, Def Leppard

66 *We grew up with Queen. Bohemian Rhapsody was like the bible for us, both in terms of the actual music and how they produced their vocals. It became a standard for us. We hope the concert will get across important information to people that know very little about aids.* 99

Def Leppard, *April 1992*

Def Leppard

Spinal Tap

Bob Geldof

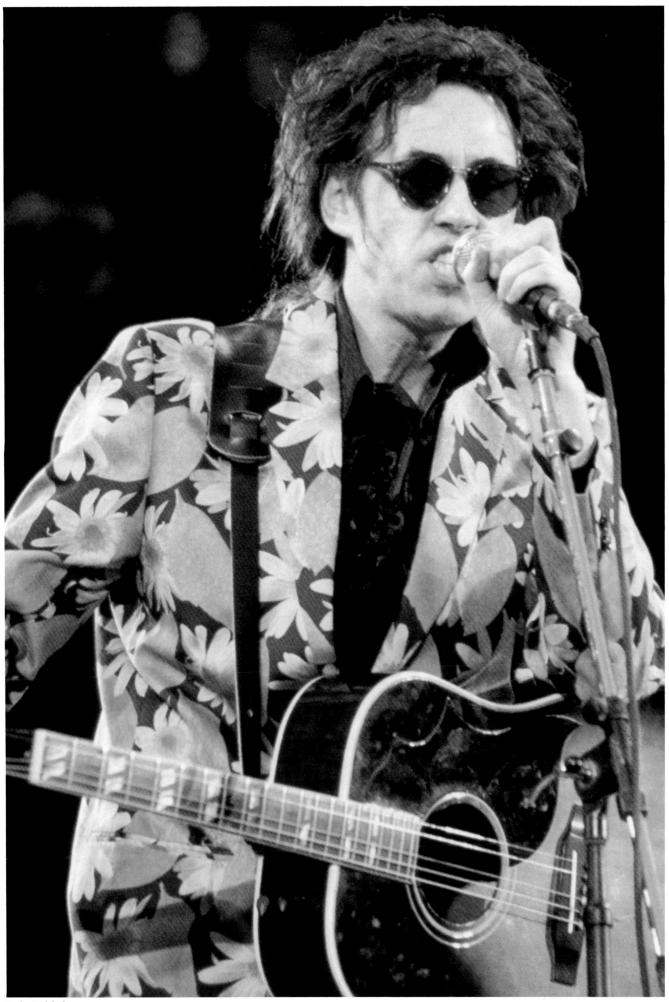

Bob Geldof

Axl Rose, Guns n' Roses

Slash, Guns n' Roses

Axl Rose

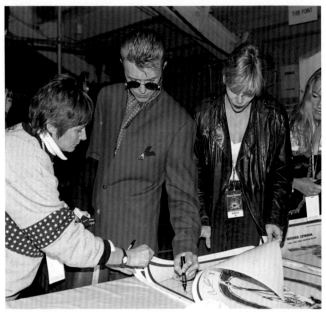

David Bowie

Elizabeth Taylor

Roger Taylor signing concert posters

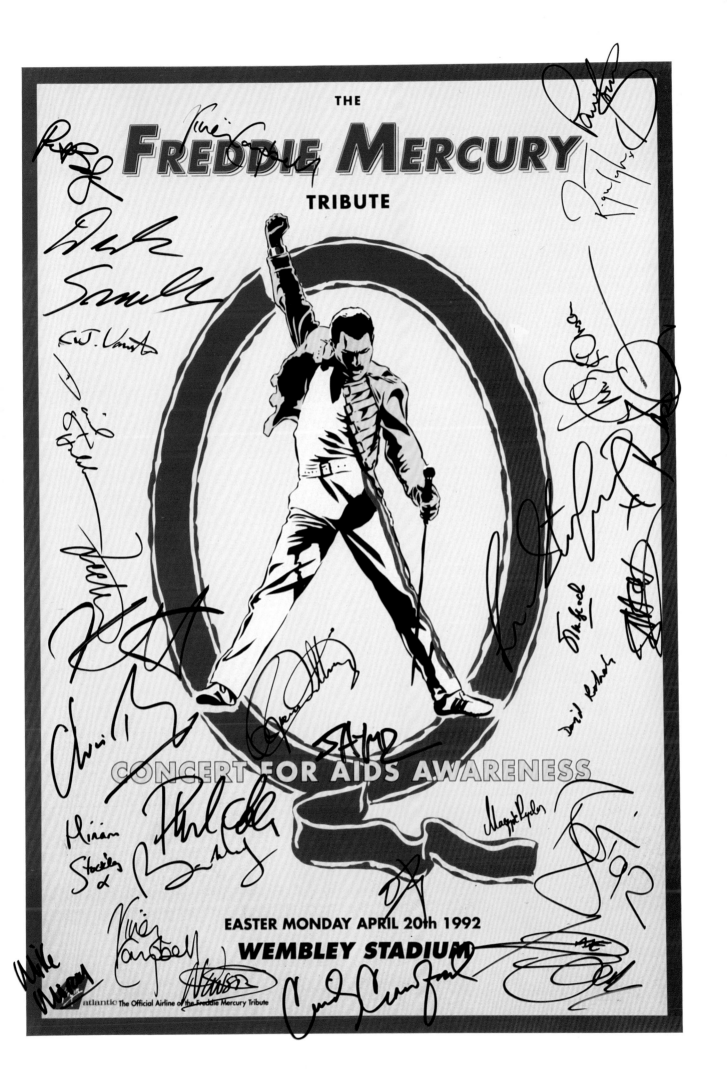

Elizabeth Taylor

" Hi, don't worry I'm not gonna sing ...

We are here to celebrate the life of Freddie Mercury. An extraordinary rock star who rushed across our cultural landscape like a comet shooting across the sky. We are here also to tell the whole world that he, like others we have lost to AIDS, died before his time.

The bright light of his talent still exhilarates us even now. That his life has been so cruelly distinguished, it needn't have happened. It shouldn't have happened. Please let's not let it happen again.

Each day around the world five thousand people are infected with HIV, the virus that causes AIDS, and just last week it was reported in the United States alone that there are nine thousand actual cases of AIDs among teenage and young adults, with thousands more that probably don't even know that they are infected.

There's seventy thousand people in this stadium tonight, look at yourselves, look at how many you are. In two short weeks there will be as many new infections as there are people here tonight. Please don't let it happen to you, you are the future, you are the best and the brightest, you are the shining lights that will illuminate a better world tomorrow.

Protect yourselves, if you have sex, every time you have sex use a condom, every single time. straight sex, gay sex, bisexual sex, use a condom, whoever you are. And if you share drugs don't share a needle.

Tonight we are here to raise money to help those living with AIDS. Tonight we are here to send them a message that we care.

But I'm also here with a message for each and every one of you, protect yourselves, love yourselves, respect yourselves. Because I will keep on telling you until you do and I won't give in and I won't give up because the world needs you to live. You see, we really love you, we really care.

God bless. **"**

Elizabeth Taylor, *20th April 1992*

Slash and Brian May

THE FREDDIE MERCURY
TRIBUTE

THE

FREDDIE
MERCURY

TRIBUTE

CONCERT FOR AIDS AWARENESS

PART
2

Slash, Joe Elliott, John Deacon, Brian May and Roger Taylor

Joe Elliott and Brian May at rehearsal

Roger Daltrey at rehearsal

Roger Daltrey

I've been a long time admirer of Queen and their music. It will be a great challenge to sing something that Freddie did so well and that's it. That's my reason for appearing.

Roger Daltrey, *April 1992*

John Deacon, Roger Daltrey, Roger Taylor and Brian May at rehearsals

Tony Iommi, Roger Daltrey and Brian May

Roger Daltrey, Brian May and Roger Taylor at rehearsals

Roger Daltrey, John Deacon and Brian May at rehearsals

Zucchero, Roger Taylor and Brian May

John Deacon and Gary Cherone

  ❝ *When Queen asked us if we*
would play the tribute, we couldn't
believe it; we still don't. Queen is
my favorite band and although
there will be millions watching,
I'll be singing to one...
He is my vocal inspiration,
my hero, Freddie Mercury.
Long may he reign! **❞**

Gary Cherone, *April 1992*

Roger Taylor

Tony Iommi

Tony Iommi and Brian May

Brian May and Robert Plant

Robert Plant

Robert Plant and Brian May

Robert Plant at rehearsal

Brian May and Mick Ronson at rehearsal

Rick Allen and James Hetfield at rehearsal

Brian May

Brian May, Elizabeth Taylor and Roger Taylor with the Freddie Mercury Quilt for the Names Project

John Deacon

Paul Young

Paul Young and Brian May

> ❝ It was a turning point for me when Freddie died, up until then I'm sorry to say I had tended to turn a blind eye to Aids, not having known anyone personally who had contracted the HIV virus. Freddie was such a part of English life that his death greatly affected me and many many other people and so when the chance came to play at Wembley, I thought yes, I want to get involved in this and do something positive for Aids awareness. ❞

Paul Young, *April 1992*

Roger Taylor

Seal

Seal at rehearsal

Seal at rehearsal

Lisa Stansfield and Brian May

Lisa Stansfield

Annie Lennox

Annie Lennox and David Bowie

David Bowie

David Bowie at rehearsal

Ian Hunter, Roger Taylor and David Bowie

Annie Lennox and Brian May

David Bowie at soundcheck

Mick Ronson at soundcheck

Ian Hunter at soundcheck

Ian Hunter, John Deacon, David Bowie and Brian May at rehearsal

Roger Taylor, George Michael and Brain May

Roger Taylor, George Michael and Brian May

George Michael, Roger Taylor and Brian May

❝ *There is something I would like to say, I think a lot of people here this evening are not necessarily people who have anything against gay people, not necessarily homophobic people, people here are probably taking some small comfort in the fact that although Freddie died of AIDS he was publicly bisexual. It's a very, very dangerous comfort. I received some figures today from AmFar, the american side of AIDS work, really. Which said the conservative estimate for the year 2000 is 40 million people on this planet will be infected by HIV and if you think, or any of you out there really think that those are all going to be gay people or drug addicts, then you are pretty well lining up to be one of those numbers. So please for God's sake and for Freddie's sake, and for your own sake, please be careful.***❞**

George Michael, *20th April 1992*

George Michael

Roger Taylor

Lisa Stansfield and George Michael

Elton John and Axl Rose

Elton John

" *Though I never met Freddie Mercury, my impression is that he was a man who loved life and lived life to the fullest of his abilities. This concert shouldn't necessarily be a mourning or a monument to Freddie, but more a celebration and a celebration of life in Freddie's honor. We're very grateful to be a part of this and hope everyone enjoys it.* "

W. Axl Rose, *April 1992*

Axl Rose and John Deacon

" *Until a cure is found I won't rest, I've lost so many friends. Becoming involved in things like this really helps to put everything in perspective. I'm in my mid forties and this is the time in life that instead of just planning everything around a career, you can try to do something else.* "

Elton John, *April 1992*

Elton John, Axl Rose, John Deacon and Brian May

Elton John at soundcheck

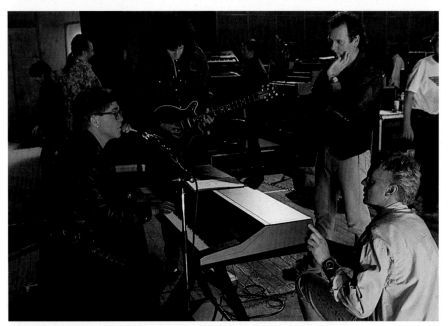

Elton John, Brian May, Spike Edney and Roger Taylor at rehearsal

Elton John and Brian May at rehearsal

" Freddie Mercury was an incredible innovative singer and frontman for a band. He was a very dear friend of mine and it was a privilege to have known him, for some of his life. He was very funny, he was extremely outrageous, he was very kind and he was a great musician, and one of the great frontmen of rock and roll bands. It's very hard to be a frontman, I mean there's not many you can think of that actually pulled it off, you can think of Jagger, you can think of Daltrey and then you can think of Freddie Mercury. And Queen were one of the bands to come out of the 70's that were so innovative, I mean when you look at videos today, Queen started videos off really. They were the people that had all the ideas to begin with. Freddie always had a sense of humour, a sense of outrage, that stole the show at Live Aid. quite simply he was one of the most important figures in rock and roll over the last twenty years. I will miss him, we will all miss him, I think, for his music and his humanity and the great thing is we still have his music to remember him by and some wonderful footage to remember that Freddie Mercury was something special. Thank you. "

Elton John, *November 1991*

Elton John

Brian May and Liza Minelli at rehearsal

Liza Minelli at rehearsal

Liza Minelli

Liza Minelli

Duff, Axl Rose, Roger Daltrey and Seal

Roger Taylor

Brian May

Brian May and George Michael

Finale

The Finale

TRIBUTE CONCERT CREDITS

Management	Jim Beach	*Management/Co-Promotion*	Queen Productions Ltd.
		Production	GLS Management Services, Inc.
Queen Productions	Julie Glover, Sally Hyatt	*Co-Promotion*	Harvey Goldsmith Entertainments,
Queen Fan Club	Jacky Gunn, Val Moss		Andrew Zweck, Danny Lawson,
		Legal Services	Lee & Thompson, Robert Lee
Production Director	Gerry Stickells	*Accounting*	Grant Thornton, Peter Chant
		International Event Publicity	Laister Dickson
Production Coordinator	Sylvia Stickells	*Publicity/Queen*	Scott Riseman Lipsey Meade
Production Assistant	Lourdes Gonzalez	*Set Design*	Planview, Inc., John McGraw
Production/Stage Manager	Rick O'Brien	*Set Construction*	Hangman, Alan Chesters
Stage Manager	Lee Charteris		Brilliant Construction, Charlie Kale
Travel Coordinator	Adrian Irvine	*Sound*	Clair Brothers Audio,
Transport Liaison	Gordon Adams		Roy Clair, Gene Clair, Greg Hall
Lighting Designer	Patrick Woodroffe	*Lighting*	Samuelson Concert Productions,
Sound Engineer	James 'Trip' Khalaf		John Coppen, Steve Moles
Monitors	Jim Devenney	*Vari*Lites*	Vari*Lite Europe, Brian Croft
Live Screen Director	Paul Becher	*Video*	Nocturne Europe Ltd.,
Site Coordinator	Graeme Fleming		Pat Morrow, Robin Coles
Staging Coordinators	Ollie Watts, Tarquin Morgan	*Screens*	Screenco Ltd., Dave Crump
Backline Coordinators	Brian 'Jobby' Zellis, Martin Groves,	*Generators*	Showpower,
	Paul 'Streaky' Hawkes		John Campion, Laurence Anderson
Sound Technicians	Dave Kob, Tom 'Duds' Ford, Keith Carrol,	*Drapes*	Acre Jean, Ross Maxwell
	Anthony Tang, Manu Dagee, Alex Broens,	*Pyrotechnics*	Le Maitre Fireworks Ltd., Wilf Scott
	Chris Lantz, Jurg Gallman	*Hire Equipment*	Sensible Music, Jeff Allen
Lighting Crew Chief	Steve Nolan	*Staging/Roofing/Trucking*	Edwin Shirley Trucking & Staging,
Lighting Board Operator	Charlie Wilson		Del Roll, Ollie Kite, Tim Norman
Lighting Technicians	Danny Nolan, Brian Condry,	*Freight*	Rock-It Cargo,Inc., David Bernstein
	Vince Foster, Barry Branford, Oliver		Rock-It Cargo Ltd., Chris Wright
	Saunders, Ray Welland, Sandford Imrie,	*Catering*	Eat Your Hearts Out!, Snakatak,
	Danny Hucklesby, Doug Brimblecombe,		Flying Saucers, Popcorn Catering
	Roger Dean, Steve Clements, Bob Batty,	*Merchandise*	Giant Merchandising,
	Paul Jennings		Peter Lubin, Steve Brickle
Vari*Lite Board Operator	Dave Hill	*Show Security*	Showsec International,
Vari*Lite Technicians	Brian Richardson, Rebecca Hughes,		Mick Upton, Gerry Slater
	Andy Doig	*Band Rehearsals*	Nomis Studios
Pyrotechnics Technician	Mick 'Shakin' McGuire	*Production Rehearsals*	Bray Film Studios
Generator Technicians	John Campion, Laurence Anderson,	*Lighting Rehearsals*	4:1 Scale Design
	Dick Ollett, Gary Rosner	*Travel Agent*	Trinifold Travel,
Sky Art Technicians	Sean Burke, Jonathan Wood		Mike and Robin Hawksworth
Band Assistant	Allistair McLaren	*Transport*	Davar Car Hire, Berryhurst,
Artist Liaison	Chris Taylor, Peter Freestone		Maxwell Car Services
Band Security	Terry Giddings, Wally Gore, John Wells	*Mobile Telephones*	Capitol Phone Hire
Chief Caterer	Kim Davenport	*Passes*	Capsulam Europe Ltd.
Merchandise	Mark Stredwick		
Charity Coordinators	Claudia Beach, Aoife O'Brien	TELEVISION	
Graphic Design	Richard Gray	*Director*	David Mallet
Event Photographer	Neal Preston	*Producers*	Queen and Jim Beach
		Production	Fugitive Television
		Executive Producers for U.S.	Tony Eaton and Kevin Wall
		Associate Director	Lauren Harris
		Production Coordinator	Gavin Taylor
		Video Inserts	DoRo Productions
		Sound Recording	David Richards
		Sound Recording Assistants	Justin Shirley-Smith, Andre Gauchat
		Mobile Recording	Manor Mobile and Radio 1
		Video Production Services	V.M. TV
		Johannesburg Satellite Insert	M-Net
		Sacramento Satellite Insert	Nocturne Productions
		International Distribution	Radio Vision International

SPECIAL THANKS TO

Dominic Anciano, Arma Andon, Audio FX, Richard Branson, Nick at Brazen Rock, Ray Burdis, Cliff Burnstein, Ernest Chapman, Roy Chapman, Debbie Cowen, Bill Curbishley, Ged Doherty, Bruce Dunbar, Michael Eisner, Tom Freston, Simon Fuller, Harvey Goldsmith, Doug Goldstein, Jeff Griffin, Stuart Grundy, The Hard Rock Cafe, Hibbert Ralph Animation Ltd., Jeff Jukes, Rob Kahane, Melanie Keady, Jamie Kellner, John Lennard, The London Monarchs, Ludwig Drums, The Mayfair Hotel, Paul McGuinness, Peter Mensch, Sally Morrison, Chris Moss, Neil Murray, The Names Project Foundation - The International Aids Memorial Quilt, Nomis Studios, Peter Paterno, The Performing Right Society for waiving their fees, Rupert Perry, Roddy Quin, Rachel Ralston, The Regents Park Hilton, John Reid, Pino Sagliocco, Joe Satriani, Harriet Sternberg, Janet Street-Porter, Jazz Summers, Tape to Tape, Elizabeth Taylor, Michele Torpedine, John Wadlow, Geoff Watchorn, Robert Urband, Vicky Vocat, Wembley Stadium, Alan Yentob, Zildjian Cymbals.
And to the BPI for letting us hijack their awards show to announce this event to the world.

TRIBUTE CONCERT SONG LIST

ENTER SANDMAN : METALLICA

SAD BUT TRUE : METALLICA

NOTHING ELSE MATTERS : METALLICA

QUEEN MEDLEY : EXTREME

MORE THAN WORDS : GARY CHERONE AND NUNO BETTENCOURT

ANIMAL : DEF LEPPARD

LET'S GET ROCKED : DEF LEPPARD

NOW I'M HERE : DEF LEPPARD AND BRIAN MAY

TOO LATE GOD : BOB GELDOF

MAJESTY OF ROCK : SPINAL TAP

PARADISE CITY : GUNS N' ROSES

KNOCKIN' ON HEAVEN'S DOOR : GUNS N' ROSES

TIE YOUR MOTHER DOWN : JOE ELLIOTT, SLASH AND QUEEN

I WANT IT ALL : ROGER DALTREY, TONY IOMMI AND QUEEN

LAS PALABRAS DE AMOR : ZUCCHERO AND QUEEN

HAMMER TO FALL : GARY CHERONE, TONY IOMMI AND QUEEN

STONE COLD CRAZY : JAMES HETFIELD, TONY IOMMI AND QUEEN

INNUENDO AND KASHMIR : ROBERT PLANT AND QUEEN

CRAZY LITTLE THING CALLED LOVE : ROBERT PLANT AND QUEEN

TOO MUCH LOVE WILL KILL YOU : BRIAN MAY

RADIO GA GA : PAUL YOUNG AND QUEEN

WHO WANTS TO LIVE FOREVER : SEAL AND QUEEN

I WANT TO BREAK FREE : LISA STANSFIELD AND QUEEN

UNDER PRESSURE : DAVID BOWIE, ANNIE LENNOX AND QUEEN

ALL THE YOUNG DUDES : IAN HUNTER, DAVID BOWIE, MICK RONSON AND QUEEN

HEROES : DAVID BOWIE, MICK RONSON AND QUEEN

YEAR OF '39 : GEORGE MICHAEL AND QUEEN

THESE ARE THE DAYS OF OUR LIVES : GEORGE MICHAEL, LISA STANSFIELD AND QUEEN

SOMEBODY TO LOVE : GEORGE MICHAEL AND QUEEN

BOHEMIAN RHAPSODY : ELTON JOHN, AXL ROSE AND QUEEN

THE SHOW MUST GO ON : ELTON JOHN, TONY IOMMI AND QUEEN

WE WILL ROCK YOU : AXL ROSE AND QUEEN

WE ARE THE CHAMPIONS : LIZA MINELLI AND CAST

SECOND HALF OF SHOW.

ADDITIONAL KEYBOARDS: SPIKE EDNEY AND MIKE MORAN. ADDITIONAL PERCUSSION: JOSH MACRAE.

ADDITIONAL VOCALS: CHRIS THOMPSON, MAGGIE RYDER, MIRIAM STOCKLEY AND THE LONDON COMMUNITY GOSPEL CHOIR.

  ❝ *I like people to go away from a Queen show feeling*
fully entertained, having had a good time. I think
Queen songs are pure escapism, like going to see a
good film – after that, they go away and say that was
great, and go back to all their problems. ❞

Freddie Mercury